W9-AMO-342

12·933397   donation
j591   Getting to know...
GET   nature's children
Vol.13

j591   j591   933397   donation
GET   GET   Getting to know...
Vol.   Vol.13   nature's children

Ge
ch

Getting To Know...

Nature's Children

MOOSE

Judy Ross

PUBLISHER	Joseph R. DeVarennes	
PUBLICATION DIRECTOR	Kenneth H. Pearson	
MANAGING EDITOR	Valerie Wyatt	
SERIES ADVISOR	Merebeth Switzer	
SERIES CONSULTANT	Michael Singleton	
CONSULTANTS	Ross James	
	Kay McKeever	
	Dr. Audrey N. Tomera	
ADVISORS	Roger Aubin	
	Robert Furlonger	
	Gaston Lavoie	
EDITORIAL SUPERVISOR	Jocelyn Smyth	
PRODUCTION MANAGER	Ernest Homewood	
PRODUCTION ASSISTANTS	Penelope Moir	
	Brock Piper	
EDITORS	Katherine Farris	Anne Minguet-Patocka
	Sandra Gulland	Sarah Reid
	Cristel Kleitsch	Cathy Ripley
	Elizabeth MacLeod	Eleanor Tourtel
	Pamela Martin	Karin Velcheff
PHOTO EDITORS	Bill Ivy	
	Don Markle	
DESIGN	Annette Tatchell	
CARTOGRAPHER	Jane Davie	
PUBLICATION ADMINISTRATION	Kathy Kishimoto	
	Monique Lemonnier	
ARTISTS	Marianne Collins	Greg Ruhl
	Pat Ivy	Mary Theberge

This series is approved and recommended by the Federation of Ontario Naturalists.

Canadian Cataloguing in Publication Data

Ross, Judy, 1942-
  Moose

(Getting to know—nature's children)
Includes index.
ISBN 0-7172-1918-6

1. Moose—Juvenile literature.
I. Title. II. Series.

QL737.U55R67 1985   j599.73'57   C85-098723-7

Have you ever wondered . . .

where moose live?	page 8
who the moose's cousins are?	page 11
if all moose have antlers?	page 11
how big a moose's antlers are?	page 12
if a moose keeps his antlers year-round?	page 15
how a moose's long legs are useful?	page 16
how a moose knows who's around?	page 19
if moose can swim?	page 20
why moose sometimes stand neck deep in water?	page 20
what is a moose's favorite food?	page 23
if moose are big eaters?	page 24
where moose sleep?	page 28
how a moose stays warm in winter?	page 28
if moose live alone or in groups?	page 31
if moose ever fight with each other?	page 31
where a female moose goes to have her babies?	page 35
how many babies a mother moose has?	page 35
what kind of sounds a baby moose makes?	page 35
when a baby moose goes for its first walk?	page 39
how a mother moose protects her babies?	page 43
what lessons a young moose has to learn?	page 44
when a young moose is ready to go off on its own?	page 46

What comes into your mind when you think of a moose? Some people think of a coatrack because the moose's upturned antlers look like a good place to hang a coat. Other people think of stilts because the moose's body is perched on top of long skinny legs.

A coatrack on stilts! If that is the way you think of moose, you are in for a surprise.

Moose may look awkward and clumsy, but don't be fooled by appearances. They are graceful, agile animals that can disappear into dense forests without making a sound. Surprised?

Few animals in North America are as impressive as a bull moose.

Awkward Beginning

For the first few days of its life a baby moose, or calf, has trouble getting around on its skinny stilt-like legs. They wobble and buckle under it, and the little moose staggers unsteadily. But the calf gets stronger and steadier on its feet every day. By the time it is a week old, the calf might be able to beat you in a race—and it is a strong swimmer too.

A calf must become strong and steady on its feet very quickly so that it can run if danger threatens. After all, it does not yet have strong legs to kick with or antlers to scare off its enemies.

Those long legs are shaky at first, but soon this young moose will be able to run faster than you can.

6

Moose Turf

Most moose live in the forested areas on the edge of the Arctic in North America and Eurasia. But some are found farther south, often near lakes or streams. Some even live in the treeless northern tundra, where the winters are often very cold.

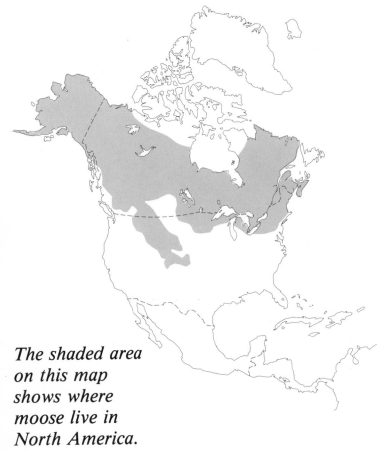

The shaded area on this map shows where moose live in North America.

You can tell this bull is a yearling by its short spiked antlers.

All in the Family

Moose are the largest members of the deer family. They are at least a head taller than their deer cousins, the elk, deer and caribou. The male, or bull, is larger than the female, or cow. He can weigh as much as 535 kilograms (1200 pounds) and stand over two metres (6 feet) tall.

How can you tell the difference between a bull and a cow moose when you cannot compare their size? It is easy. Only the male moose have antlers.

Even though the female is smaller than the male, she still is as large as a horse!

Heavy Headed

Imagine having to walk, run and even swim with a piano bench tied to your head. Sound impossible? Not for a bull moose. A fully grown bull moose's antlers can be about the size and weight of a piano bench. But while you might have trouble carrying around something so large and heavy, the moose does not even seem to notice its cumbersome headgear. It can lope easily through dense forest without smashing its antlers into trees or getting them stuck in branches.

Male moose do not start life with a handsome pair of antlers. During their first year they grow tiny brown buttons. The next year their antlers are a bit bigger. They stick out on either side of the moose's head like handles. Finally, after seven years of bigger and bigger antlers, the male's headgear is fully grown. This may seem like a long wait for a pair of antlers, but it is just as well. Imagine what a mess a young moose would be in if it suddenly sprouted a pair of antlers the size of a piano bench.

Something's Missing

Male moose do not have antlers all year round. In early winter their antlers drop off. Sometimes one antler is shed before the other, and the moose must get used to being lopsided for a few days.

In early spring a new set of antlers sprouts. First tiny black knobs appear. These knobs are covered with a soft fuzzy skin, called velvet. This velvet contains blood vessels to nourish the antlers and help them to grow.

By mid-July, the antlers are full size, and in early fall the velvet begins to fall off. During this stage the moose looks very messy. It has strips of ragged velvet hanging from his headgear. To help loosen this fuzzy skin, the moose often rubs his antlers against trees.

Comparison of moose and elk antlers.

moose

elk

Shreds of torn velvet still cling to the antlers of this moose.

The Big Stretch

A moose is so tall that the average three-year-old child would only reach its knobby knees. Its long thin legs account for most of its height. Having long legs is a big advantage for a forest dweller. They make it possible for the moose to step easily over logs on the ground, reach up into trees for food and wade through deep snow that would stop other animals.

If you are ever lucky enough to see a moose in the wild, stop and watch how it moves through the forest. It majestically strides through the trees and over fallen logs without slowing its pace. A moose on the move is a very graceful creature indeed.

The moose's long legs are also useful when it needs to defend itself or escape. It can kick out to fend off a hungry wolf or, if that fails, outrun its attackers.

Like other members of the deer family, the moose has split hoofs for feet. These spread out slightly as it walks over swampy ground to provide more support for its big, bulky body.

Opposite page:

If threatened, a moose will kick out with either its front or hind hoofs—and it doesn't often miss its target!

16

Sight, Sounds and Scents

Those sleepy looking big brown eyes may be one of the most handsome features of a moose, but they are not very useful. A moose has very poor eyesight. Luckily its other senses are much sharper.

Its big ears are like those of a mule. Whenever a moose hears something that may mean danger, its ears stand up on end to catch the sound waves. Thanks to these effective sound catchers a moose can hear much better than we can.

A moose uses its big nose to sniff the air. Its keen sense of smell can pick up the wind-blown scent of other animals long before it can see them.

Who goes there?

Moose tracks

Water Lover

Moose like to be near water where they can find food and escape from danger. They are strong swimmers and have even been known to dive underwater in search of a tasty plant. When a moose dives underwater, its nostrils close to keep the water out, just as a submarine's hatches close before submerging.

A river or lake is also a handy refuge from black flies and mosquitoes. In summer a moose will stand neck deep in water so that these pesky insects cannot bite it.

Moose are usually seen in or near water.

Big Eaters

It sometimes seems that a moose's day is just one long meal. In summer, juicy green leaves, twigs and plants make up most of its diet, but its favorite food is water lilies. Much of a moose's water lily eating takes place in the early morning or late in the afternoon. The moose stands partially submerged in the water and dips its nose under to tear off the lilies.

This bull didn't have to wade in very deep to find a choice supply of tender treats.

In winter, when water plants are not available, the moose eats more twigs. A full-grown moose may munch down 18 to 23 kilograms (40-50 pounds) of twigs a day. At the end of the winter, when the moose has already eaten most of the twigs it can reach, it may tear strips of bark off trees and eat that.

It is easy to tell if a moose has been feeding nearby. The trees will be twigless up to a height of several metres (yards). That is as high as a hungry moose can reach.

The word moose is an Algonkian Indian word which means "twig eater."

Cud Chewers

Like all of its deer family relatives, a moose is a cud chewer. This means it chomps down food while wandering around, but waits until it can rest quietly before it chews it properly. It can do this because part of its stomach acts as a "storage tank" for unchewed food. When it rests, it brings the food or cud from this storage tank into its mouth. Then it can chew in peace. On a hot summer day a moose often lies down in a shady spot to chew its cud; in winter, it may flop down in the snow.

Maple on the menu.

Winter Woolies

Many animals build nests or dig burrows or dens for homes. Not the moose. It wanders from place to place in search of food and sleeps wherever it is. That may sound fine in summer, but what happens in winter?

Although the moose does not have a den to snuggle up in, it has no problem staying warm. It grows a thick two-layered fur coat in the late fall. Long guard hairs shed ice and snow and keep out the cold winds, while a layer of thick underfur keeps the moose's body heat from escaping into the cold air.

The moose calf stays by its mother's side for protection.

933897

Moose Groups

Moose live alone most of the year, but sometimes in winter they gather in small groups to search for food. They scratch at the snow with their hoofed front legs to dig out bits of plants or roots. It does not take long before the snow gets tramped down by a group of moose. These flattened areas are called "yards." But even in yards the moose keep their distance. They may feed near each other, but the strongest and largest always gets the first and best food.

Mating Season

Moose mate in the fall. Their courtship is a noisy and sometimes even dangerous affair. To let a male know she is interested, the female bellows loudly. If two males hear her call, the trouble starts. The two bulls may fight to win her. These "bullfights" often involve much clanging and smashing of antlers. But usually the weaker bull backs off before anyone gets hurt.

Opposite page:
Two's company.

Overleaf:
It's a head-on collision when two bull moose rivals meet.

A Moose Nursery

In the spring, the cow moose goes off by herself to find a place to give birth to her calves. She is very fussy about a birth place. It must be well hidden from predators, so she looks for a spot among bushes and trees, usually at the water's edge where the trees are dense. An island is a good, safe birth place. In this safe, hidden spot, the cow gives birth to her calves. Usually she has twins, but sometimes as many as three or possibly only one.

A newborn moose calf weighs 10 to 16 kilograms (22-35 pounds)—about the weight of a large dog. The first sounds that it utters are low grunts, but soon it is calling loudly to its mother with a sound much like a human baby's cry.

Taking it easy.

From Wobble to Walk

For a few days the baby calf lies
on the soft ground in the secret
hiding place, sleeping and nursing
on its mother's milk. At first, the
mother cuddles and nuzzles her
calf with her soft, rubbery nose.
But soon she begins to nudge it to
get up and walk.

*During the first year of its life the
mother moose and calf are seldom
apart.*

36

First Outing

When it is about three days old the calf is ready to venture out for a walk with its mother. It wobbles unsteadily behind her as she browses for food near thick bushes. If danger approaches she will nudge the calf into the bushes, out of sight.

Before long the calf will begin nibbling on tender shoots and young buds on the bushes and trees, and by fall it will no longer need to drink its mother's milk.

After a shaky first two weeks, the young moose gets more sure-footed every day.

Young Swimmer

If you ever see two moose swimming, look closely. One is probably a baby moose. A moose calf can swim when it is only a few days old, but it is not yet a strong swimmer. From time to time it may rest its chin on its mother's back until it has enough strength to paddle on its own again.

Quite at home in the water, the moose is a powerful swimmer.

40

Wolves and bears see small moose calves as tasty dinners. So the mother moose must be especially alert to protect her calf. She relies on her keen senses of smell and hearing to alert her to any approaching danger.

If her calf is threatened, the cow moose lowers her head and snorts loudly like a horse. Then she may rear up on her hind legs and paw the air. If all this does not frighten off the enemy, she will kick out with her long, strong legs and sharp front hoofs. A moose can cripple a wolf with one well-placed kick.

If the calf's own father comes near, he will get the same treatment as other intruders.

This young calf will stay with its mother for at least one year before venturing off on its own.

Survival Lessons

Moose in the wild may live to be 20 years old, but there are many dangers and hardships to be faced along the way. During its time with its mother, the calf learns all of the lessons it will need to survive. It watches how its mother pulls up tender water lilies and then it does the same thing. It sees which trees have good twigs and bark by watching her too. And, if danger threatens, it learns how to fight off enemies. It even learns how to escape pesky flies and mosquitoes by hiding in the water. All of these lessons are important for the young calf. Only by learning them well will it survive.

Leaving Home

The moose calf grows quickly, and by its second spring it is ready to go off on its own. When it leaves, its mother begins to search for a hiding place for another set of new babies.

A female calf can be a mother herself at age three. A male calf will not mate until he is five or six. That is when his antlers will be full-grown and he will be able to challenge other males in a mating contest. Until then the young moose will live alone, wandering through the forest, stopping now and then for a cooling dip in a lake or a snack of delicious water lilies.

Words to Know

Antlers   Hard, bony growths on the head of male moose.

Bull   Male moose.

Cow   Female moose.

Cud   Hastily swallowed food brought back for chewing by cud chewers such as deer, cows and moose.

Hoofs   Feet of moose, cattle, deer and some other animals.

Mating season   The time of year when animals come together to produce young.

Nostrils   The openings in the nose that let air in.

Tundra   Flat land in the Arctic where no trees grow.

Velvet   Soft skin which covers moose's antlers while they grow.

Yard   An area where moose gather in winter to find food.

INDEX

antlers, 5, 11, 12, 15, 46

baby. *See* calf
bears, 43
bull, 11, 12, 31, 43

calf, 6, 35, 36, 39, 40, 43, 44, 46
caribou, 11
communication, 31
cow, 11, 31, 35, 37, 39, 40, 43, 44, 46
cud, 27

danger, 6, 16, 19, 39, 43, 44
defense, 16, 43
description, 5, 11
diet, 23, 24, 39, 44
distribution, 8
diving, 20

elk, 11
eyes, 19

female. *See* cow
fighting, 31

getting along, 31
groups, 31
growing up, 43, 44, 46
guard hairs, 28

habitat, 8, 16, 20
homes, 28, 35
hoofs, 16, 31, 43

legs, 5, 6, 16, 39, 43
locomotion, 5, 12, 16, 39

male. *See* bull
mating season, 31
mosquitoes, 20, 44

nose, 19, 20, 36
nostrils, 20

relatives, 11, 16, 27

senses
  hearing, 19, 43
  sight, 19
  smell, 19, 43
size, 11
snow, 16, 27, 28, 31
sounds, 31, 35, 43
spring, 15, 35, 46
summer, 15, 23, 28
swimming, 6, 12, 20, 40

territory, 31
tracks
  illus. 19
twigs, 23, 24

underfur, 28

velvet, 15

water lilies, 23, 44, 46
winter, 24, 27, 28, 31
wolves, 43

yarding, 31

Cover Photo: J.D. Markou (Valan Photos)

Photo Credits: Brian Milne (First Light Associated Photographers), pages 4, 14; Murray O'Neill (Valan Photos), pages 7, 38; Bill Ivy, pages 9, 10, 17, 18, 26; Brian Milne (Valan Photos), page 13; Joseph R. Pearce (Valan Photos), page 21; Arthur Savage, page 22; Vince Claerhout, page 25; Dennis W. Schmidt (Valan Photos), page 29: J.D. Markou (Valan Photos), pages 30, 41; Thomas Kitchin (Valan Photos), pages 32-33; Stephen J. Krasemann (Valan Photos), pages 34, 36, 42; Wayne Lankinen (Valan Photos), page 45.

Getting To Know...

Nature's Children

DOWNY WOODPECKER

Katherine Grier

PUBLISHER	Joseph R. DeVarennes
PUBLICATION DIRECTOR	Kenneth H. Pearson
MANAGING EDITOR	Valerie Wyatt
SERIES ADVISOR	Merebeth Switzer
SERIES CONSULTANT	Michael Singleton
CONSULTANTS	Ross James
	Kay McKeever
	Dr. Audrey N. Tomera
ADVISORS	Roger Aubin
	Robert Furlonger
	Gaston Lavoie
EDITORIAL SUPERVISOR	Jocelyn Smyth
PRODUCTION MANAGER	Ernest Homewood
PRODUCTION ASSISTANTS	Penelope Moir
	Brock Piper
EDITORS	Katherine Farris	Anne Minguet-Patocka
	Sandra Gulland	Sarah Reid
	Cristel Kleitsch	Cathy Ripley
	Elizabeth MacLeod	Eleanor Tourtel
	Pamela Martin	Karin Velcheff
PHOTO EDITORS	Bill Ivy
	Don Markle
DESIGN	Annette Tatchell
CARTOGRAPHER	Jane Davie
PUBLICATION ADMINISTRATION	Kathy Kishimoto
	Monique Lemonnier
ARTISTS	Marianne Collins	Greg Ruhl
	Pat Ivy	Mary Theberge

This series is approved and recommended by the Federation of Ontario Naturalists.

Canadian Cataloguing in Publication Data

Grier, Katherine
  Downy woodpecker

(Getting to know—nature's children)
Includes index.
ISBN 0-7172-1922-4

1. Woodpeckers—Juvenile literature.
I. Title. II. Series.

QL696.P56G74 1985   j598'.72   C85-098710-5

Have you ever wondered . . .

how to recognize a Downy Woodpecker?   page 9

where Downy Woodpeckers live?   page 12

if the Downy is a friendly neighbor?   page 15

what Downy Woodpeckers eat?   page 16

how a Downy taps for its meals?   page 19

how many times a minute a Downy taps?   page 20

why so much tapping doesn't hurt the Downy's head?   page 20

how many toes a Downy has?   page 23

how a Downy uses its tail?   page 23

how a Downy takes care of its feathers?   page 24

if a Downy's feathers wear out?   page 24

what Downy Woodpeckers do in winter?   page 27

if Downy Woodpeckers take baths?   page 28

how a Downy lets other birds know how it feels?   page 31

how a Downy finds a mate?   page 35

how long it takes Downy Woodpeckers to make a nest?   page 37

how many eggs the Downy mother lays?   page 39

what Downy Woodpecker eggs look like?   page 39

how long it takes Downy eggs to hatch?   page 39

what a newly hatched Downy looks like?   page 40

if Downy Woodpeckers are good parents?   page 40

when a young Downy is ready for life on its own?   page 42

Downy Woodpeckers

Have you ever heard a busy drumming sound coming from a nearby pole or tree? Did you follow it, trying to find out exactly where the sound was coming from? If you did, you might have seen a small, red-headed bird rapping into the wood with its bill. Yes, to us that rapping sound means, "Look, and you'll see a woodpecker!"

Perhaps you've wondered what a woodpecker is doing when it raps or pecks. Why doesn't all that knocking with its bill hurt its head? Maybe you've even thought that woodpeckers weren't quite like other birds—and you would be right.

Woodpeckers are specially suited to life in the trees. We'll find out how by looking at one kind of woodpecker that you are likely to see in your neighborhood, whether you live in the country, town or city. It is a small, lively woodpecker that is not afraid of people. It is called the Downy Woodpecker.

A Long Way Down

A young Downy Woodpecker pokes its head out of the hole in the tree where it was born. It is hungry, but it cannot fly yet. So it is looking for its mother and father who usually feed it. Behind it in the nest, its brothers and sisters call out hungrily too. Where is dinner?

The young Downy sees its parents perched on a distant branch. Why aren't they coming with food? Then suddenly a fly buzzes past. The hungry young Downy cannot resist it. It reaches out to grab this tasty bug snack in its bill and . . . pop! It is out of the nest and fluttering down to the ground. It is the young Downy's first flight!

The Downy Woodpecker parents look on from their perch. They know their young will not leave the nest unless they have good reason to do so. And what better reason is there than food? They watch for the next hungry young bird to try its wings.

Young Downy Woodpeckers.

Downy Relatives

The Downy Woodpecker belongs to a big family. There are 179 different kinds of woodpeckers living around the world. Twenty-two kinds live in North America, and the Downy is one of them.

All woodpeckers have several things in common. They are all good climbers. They all use their bills to poke or dig for their food. And they all can use their bills to make holes for their nests as well.

Just as people look different, so do the Downy's relatives. Some are as big as crows, while others are as tiny as sparrows. Some have bright green feathers, while others are black and white. There are woodpeckers of many other colors as well.

The different kinds of woodpeckers like different things to eat. Many eat insects they find on the ground or in trees. Some lap up the sap that flows from holes they make in tree trunks. And others prefer acorns, storing a supply for the winter in holes they dig in the bark of a tree.

Getting to Know the Downy

The Downy Woodpecker is a small woodpecker. It only weighs about 28 grams (1 ounce) when fully grown. This is about as much as an eraser weighs. The Downy measures about 15 centimetres (6 inches) from its head to the tip of its tail.

The Downy is a handsome bird. It has a bright white chest and a white stripe down its back. It has black wings with white checks and stripes. And the male has a small red patch on the back of its head. The same patch on the female is black or white.

Copycat Cousin

The Downy's distinctive markings should make it easy to recognize. But there is one problem. One of its cousins, the Hairy Woodpecker, has almost the same markings. If you could put a Downy and a Hairy Woodpecker side by side, you would see that the Hairy Woodpecker is much bigger. But since you usually see a woodpecker on its own, this "size test" does not always work.

The best way to tell if a woodpecker is a Downy is to look at its bill. The Hairy Woodpecker's bill is as long as its head, while the Downy Woodpecker's bill is much shorter—about half that length.

Compare this Hairy Woodpecker's bill with that of the Downy. Unlike most woodpeckers, the Downy has quite a short and stubby bill.

At Home on its Range

Downy Woodpeckers live all over North America—that is, wherever there are trees. They make their homes in city parks and backyards, farm orchards and open woodlands.

Every Downy lives on its own range—a large area of land that gives the Downy its food and shelter. In it there are sure to be deciduous trees—trees that lose their leaves in the fall—where the Downy can find insects and grubs to eat. And there will also be dead or dying trees in which the Downy can chisel out a roosting hole to sleep in or a nest hole for its young.

In spring and summer, the Downy shares a range with a mate and raises a family. In fall and winter it lives alone on its own range. The Downy lives on the same range year after year. It gets to know where favorite trees or stumps are, how to get from one spot to another and where the best eating and hiding places are.

Only the males have a patch of red on their heads.

A Friendly Neighbor?

In fall and winter when the Downy lives by itself, it does not get upset if other birds come into its range. In fact, being a small woodpecker among many larger birds, it sometimes does not have much choice.

The Downy and the Hairy Woodpeckers— who look so much alike—sometimes even share the same trees. The larger Hairy Woodpecker searches the main trunk for food and uses its longer, stronger bill to chisel holes in hard live wood. The smaller Downy Woodpecker finds soft dead limbs to dig holes in. It moves easily among the smaller branches looking for insects near the bark's surface. Because the two woodpeckers look for food in different places, the Downy and the Hairy live side by side in peace. A Downy will also share its range with another Downy.

But when a Downy couple start making their nest and getting ready to raise a family, watch out. They are no longer friendly neighbors. In fact they want to be left alone and will drive other birds, even other Downy Woodpeckers, out of their range.

A Downy Diet

The Downy gets much of its food by eating insects that crawl on the bark of a tree. Many insects can move fast, but so can the Downy. It hops quickly over its favorite feeding places—small trees and the upper branches and twigs of big trees—snatching bugs where it finds them. Its favorites are beetles, beetle larvae, ants, caterpillars and other small insects.

The Downy eats some fruits and berries too, when it can find them—raspberries, blackberries, cherries and even the berries of poison ivy and poison sumac. It will also drink sap from the holes that its relative, the Sapsucker Woodpecker, taps deep into live trees.

The Downy's eating habits change with the seasons. In spring and summer there are lots of insects, and it can eat well just by looking for them on top of the bark. But in fall and winter, it must get insects that live under the tree bark, and so it must tap for its meal.

Unlike other woodpeckers the Downy will hunt for food in smaller scrub and bushes.

16

Tapping for Food

How does the Downy get at insects that live in tunnels in tree wood or telephone poles? First it chisels into the wood to open up the tunnels. It does this by hammering its straight sharp bill into the wood over and over again. Although the Downy's bill is made mostly of hard bone, it is not as long or strong as many other woodpecker's bills. So it usually digs into softer dead or dying wood for an insect dinner.

Getting the insects out of their tunnel homes is no problem either. It uses its tongue to "fish" them out. The Downy's tongue is long enough to probe deep into the insects' tunnels. On the tip of its tongue are tiny barbs that work like a fishhook. When the Downy catches an insect, the barbs hold it fast. Its tongue is also sticky, and this helps hold the insect too. Then the Downy draws its tongue back into its bill with the bug attached.

A Protected Body

Would you rather catch a baseball with your bare hand or a padded glove? Probably a padded glove. The Downy uses padding too. It drums its bill against a tree over 100 times a minute. But its head does not get hurt because it is protected—just as your hand is protected by a baseball glove. The Downy's bill is wide at the base, the bones of its skull are thick and heavy, and the muscles around its head and neck are strong. Together, the bill, skull and muscles spread and absorb the force of the blows to protect the Downy's head from injury.

When the Downy chisels into a tree trunk, the air is filled with fine powder and flying chips of wood. You would think that its nostrils would get clogged, and that it would have a hard time breathing. But the Downy's nostrils, which are at the base of its bill, are covered with fine feathers. These feathers work as a filter and keep out all the wood dust, so that it breathes in only clear air.

The Downy leans on its tail for extra support.

20

Tree Top Eating

Holding onto a tree and eating at the same time might not sound like your idea of a picnic, but it is a snap for a Downy.

Like most woodpeckers, the Downy is well-equipped for climbing straight up trees. It has four long toes on each foot, two pointing forward and two backward. Each toe ends in a sharp, curved nail that gives the Downy a good grip.

The Downy's tail also helps it both when it is climbing and when it stops to eat. The feathers in its tail are pointed and stiff. The Downy leans back against these stiff tail feathers and uses them as a prop.

Two pairs of toes, one pointing forward and the other back, give the Downy a very firm grip.

The rough bark shown here is easy for a Downy to cling to.

Keeping Clean

The Downy works hard, but it also takes time to relax. Preening and keeping its feathers well tended is one way the Downy takes it easy. Each Downy has a special high stump or tree branch that is its favorite preening place.

There it uses its bill to poke deep down among its feathers, cleaning away dirt and tiny parasites. It straightens some feathers by pulling them carefully through its bill. In between preening, the Downy shrugs its shoulders, fluffing and lifting its feathers before flattening them out again.

No matter how carefully a woodpecker takes care of its feathers, a year's wear-and-tear makes them worn and ragged. And so each summer, the Downy molts—it grows a new set of feathers. The old ones fall out little by little, so that the Downy is never bald. It always has enough feathers to go about its work as the new feathers grow in.

A downy's molt is so gradual it almost passes unnoticed.

Going South?

When winter sets in, most Downy Woodpeckers stay on their own ranges. Their roosting holes are little caves in wood that protect them from the wind, snow and rain. Using their bills, they can tap for insects from inside their cave.

But Downy Woodpeckers that live in places that get very cold or snowy in the winter cannot always find enough to eat. They fly to warmer places where they are sure to find food. Some just move down a mountainside to a protected valley, while others fly farther south.

One bird-watcher found that some Downy Woodpeckers who usually flew south stayed on their ranges all winter when she put suet feeders out for them. The suet was the extra food they needed for the winter.

Some Downy Woodpeckers shift southward in the fall to avoid the colder regions.

Two Kinds of Baths

Downy Woodpeckers do not like water very much, but they do take an occasional bath in the snow. On a warm, sunny day in late winter, you might find one dipping its bill into the wet snow, scooping the snow over its shoulder and flapping its wings to spread it around.

There is one kind of bath that Downy Woodpeckers really like—a sunbath. A Downy will sprawl along a branch, facedown, with its wings spread half-open. It lifts the feathers on its shoulders and neck, sticks its feet straight back out from under it and soaks in the sun's rays.

Warm rays of the sun are a welcomed treat during the long winter.

Woodpecker Talk

The Downy does not "sing" as many birds do. But it does make sounds and movements that tell other birds how it feels and what it is going to do. Some of a Downy's calls are loud and some are soft, others are angry, frightened or happy. Its loud "thick" call says, "Here I am," and can be heard a long way off. A sharp "tick-tick-tick" call says, "I'm a little scared." A loud "tickirrr" call says, "Danger!" A soft "tut-tit-wi-tut-it" call says, "Hello," or, "It's good to be with you."

Sounds are not the Downy's only way of "talking." It also raises and lowers its feathers and flies or moves in different ways to send messages. If a Downy wants to say, "This is my tree. Stay away," it stretches out its head and neck, points its bill into the air and whips its head from side to side. To other birds, the message is clear.

Forest Drums

The Downy does not tap on wood only to find food. Sometimes it uses its bill like a drumstick to rap out messages on favorite hollow posts and trees. It drums in steady bursts. It can rattle off 10 hits in a row and then do it again and again, perhaps 15 times in a minute. In this way it sends messages:

"I'm looking for a mate!"

"This is my part of the woods!"

"I'm over here!"

The rapid tapping of the Downy can be heard for quite a distance.

Time for a Mate

In late winter or early spring, the Downy knows it is time to raise a family. The female begins to look for a mate. She drums out a message and if a male hears her, he drums back.

Before they settle down as a pair, the two Downy Woodpeckers do a lot of drumming back and forth. They also strut around with their feathers fluffed out, and visit nest holes from past years. All this helps them decide to stop living alone and start a family.

Downy Woodpeckers mate for life. They nest on the same range, usually the male's, year after year. But because they live alone the rest of the year, even Downy Woodpeckers who have mated before must get to know each other all over again at the beginning of each nesting season.

Few woodpeckers perch crosswise on a branch like the one shown here. The Downy is the exception.

Hard-working Nest Builders

Downy Woodpeckers dig out a new nest hole each year. They each tap at many different trees before choosing a new site—but the female has the final say.

Downy Woodpeckers dig their holes high above the ground in dead wood. Often the female will choose a dead tree branch, a tall fence post or a telephone pole. The male does most of the chiseling and the female helps. The Downy will dig for about 15 minutes at a time and then take a break to rest or eat before going back to work again.

The Downy Woodpeckers work hard, but they also work carefully. First they dig a small cone in the middle of the spot that will be the "front door." As the hole gets deeper, the digging Downy must wiggle out backward, its feathers all ruffled, to toss a bill-full of wood chips over its shoulder.

Snug and Safe

When the Downy Woodpeckers are finished, they have a nest that will shelter them and their young from bad weather and keep them safe from most enemies. The entrance hole is just big enough to let a grown-up Downy pass through. A passage leads straight in, then drops down to a wide nest hole. A few wood chips are left inside to make the floor soft enough for a nest.

Downy Woodpeckers take about two weeks to dig out their nest hole. But if other birds drive them away close to egg-laying time, they can dig a new nest in two days of *very* hard work.

In between digging, the Downy Woodpeckers drum out the message that the small territory around their nest tree belongs to them and nobody else. And they drive away any bird who comes too close.

Cut-away of a Downy's nest hole.

A Family on the Way

The Downy female usually lays four or five small eggs. They are pure white, unlike many birds'eggs that are colored or mottled to blend in with the world around them. Because the Downy's eggs are out of sight inside the nest hole, special coloring is not needed to keep them from being seen.

The Downy takes four to six days to lay her eggs. Once she is finished, a peaceful time begins. For 12 days, until the eggs begin to hatch, both parents take long turns keeping the eggs warm and covered. During the whole 12 days, the eggs are never left uncovered for more than a few minutes.

Busy with Babies

The Downy nestlings are blind, featherless and hungry when they hatch. Their parents take turns feeding them. They bring food to the nest every two or three minutes all through the day. While one parent searches for food, the other usually stays with the babies, protecting them and comforting them with soft calls.

At first the parent brings one or two very small ants. It climbs right down into the nesting hole with this snack to feed one helpless baby at a time. But within a week, the nestlings are strong enough to climb the nest walls and meet their parent halfway. By this time they have moved onto big insects. Before long they are chippering loudly at the nest's entrance as they wait for the next delivery of food.

Until the young are grown, the father spends his nights in the nest while the mother sleeps nearby in another roosting hole. The father keeps the nest clean. The babies' droppings come out in tough clean sacks that the father picks up in his bill and dumps outside.

Finding Their Wings

After three weeks of hard work, the Downy Woodpecker parents know that it is almost time for their young to leave the nest. The young woodpeckers are almost as big as their parents and have grown a full set of feathers.

The adults encourage the young ones to leave. They begin to spend much of their time outside the nest. And they bring food only about three times an hour instead of 15 times. At last hunger overcomes the young woodpeckers' fear of flying and soon they are as graceful in the air as their parents.

Not quite ready to fly . . . but it won't be long.

On Their Own

Once the young Downy Woodpeckers have left the nest, they never return to it. Each sleeps alone, hidden among the leaves of a nearby tree.

But they are far from ready for life on their own. Though they learn to fly and climb up trees very quickly, learning to feed themselves takes another three weeks. During that time, their parents help feed them. They find their young by following their calls. Those who are closest or call loudest get fed first.

As the young Downy Woodpeckers get better and better at looking after themselves, the family begins to move apart. By the middle of the summer, the young birds have grown up. They fly off to find ranges of their own and to dig a roosting hole for the coming winter.

As for their parents, they return to their own separate ranges. There they take up their solitary fall and winter ways until spring draws them together again.

Feeding so many young keeps both mom and dad very busy.

A Downy Long Life

The Downy, like most woodpeckers, is a tough bird. It is most in danger when it is young—as an egg, a nestling or a very young bird without a roosting hole. Then animals small enough to sneak into a Downy Woodpecker hole (such as a red squirrel) and hunting birds (such as a hawk) may try to make it into a tender meal.

But the Downy really has few enemies. If it survives the early days, it is quite likely to live to Downy old age—about eight or nine years old. That is not so surprising. After all, the Downy carries all the tools it needs to take care of itself in its life in the trees.

Special Words

Larvae The second stage of an insect's life, after it has hatched out of the egg.

Markings Patterns and colors in fur and feathers.

Mate To come together to produce young. Also either member of an animal pair.

Molt To shed feathers or fur from time to time.

Nest hole A hole dug in a tree by a Downy Woodpecker for a nest.

Nestling A young bird that has not yet left the nest.

Nostrils Openings in the nose or bill that allow air into the body.

Parasite A plant or animal that lives on another.

Preening Grooming of feathers with the bill.

Range Area that an animal or group of animals lives in and often defends from other animals.

Roosting hole A hole in a tree where a Downy Woodpecker sleeps at night.

INDEX

babies. *See* nestlings
bill, 8, 11, 19, 20, 24, 32, 36
brooding, 39

climbing, 23
communication, 31, 32, 35, 45
construction, 8, 12, 20, 36

description, 5, 9, 11, 19, 23
diet, 6, 12, 15, 16, 27
distribution, 11, 12

eggs, 39, 46
enemies, 46

fall, 12, 15, 16, 45
family, 6, 12, 15, 35, 39, 40, 42
feathers, 20, 23, 24, 42
feeding, 8, 12, 15, 16, 19, 23, 27, 40, 42
feet, 23
female, 9, 35, 36, 39
flying, 31

getting along, 12, 15, 35, 45
growing up, 6, 40, 42, 45, 46

habitat, 5, 12
Hairy Woodpecker, 11, 15
head, 20
home, 12, 37

keeping clean, 24, 28, 40
keeping warm, 27, 28

lifespan, 46
locomotion, 8, 16, 23, 31

male, 9, 35, 36, 40
mating, 35
migration, 27
molting, 24

nest, 6, 12, 27, 36, 37
nestlings, 6, 40, 42, 45, 46
nostrils, 20

preening, 24
protection, 12, 20, 27, 31, 37, 39, 40, 45

relatives, 8, 11, 15, 16

Sapsucker Woodpecker, 16
sense of touch, 19
size, 11
sleeping, 45
spring, 12, 16, 35
summer, 12, 16, 45

tail, 23
tapping, 20, 32, 36
territory, 12, 15, 27, 31, 35, 37, 45
toes, 23
tongue, 19

wings, 31
winter, 12, 15, 16, 27, 35, 45

Cover Photo: Robert McCaw (Network Stock Photo File)

Photo Credits: Brian Morin (Network Stock Photo File), page 4; Michel Bourque (Valan Photos), pages 7, 43; Bill Ivy, pages 10, 13, 26; Harold V. Green (Valan Photos), page 14; Robert McCaw (Network Stock Photo File), pages 17, 30, 34; Stephen J. Krasemann (Valan Photos), page 18; National Museum of Natural Science, page 21; James M. Richards, pages 22, 29, 44; Robert C. Simpson (Valan Photos), page 25; Barry Griffiths (Network Stock Photo File), page 34; Wayne Lankinen (Valan Photos), pages 38, 41.